Quality
in the
Public Sector

Second Edition

Essential Skills for the Public Sector

HB PUBLICATIONS

Jennifer Bean
Lascelles Hussey

HB PUBLICATIONS
(Incorporated as Givegood Limited)

Published by:

HB Publications
London, England

First Published 1998 © HB Publications
Second Edition 2011 © HB Publications

British Library Cataloguing in Publication Data

ISBN 978-1899448-82-1

For further information see www.hbpublications.com
and www.fci-system.com

Contents

Chapter 1

Introduction

Quality is a major issue for all organisations striving towards continuous improvement. Quality issues have become extremely important in the public sector, as governments around the world place increasing emphasis on the quality of outputs and outcomes from public services. Public sector managers are tasked with the responsibility of delivering high quality services, often within tight financial constraints, with the aim of achieving the best possible value for money.

The key questions facing managers with respect to quality are:

- *How do we define it? (Particularly as some public sector services are intangible in nature.)*
- *How do we measure it?*
- *How do we monitor it? And*
- *How do we manage it?*

These questions are complicated by the need to become more customer focused, as views on quality are not the sole domain of those delivering the service, but also those receiving it.

Quality in the Public Sector seeks to demystify many of the issues surrounding quality in public sector environments. It provides techniques for setting quality standards, measuring and monitoring quality and identifying the costs and benefits of implementing quality management. It also addresses some of the difficulties in trying to maintain or improve quality standards in a climate of constrained or shrinking financial resources.

It is increasingly common for public sector organisations to seek recognition for having a quality service, and there are a number of quality kite marks that can be achieved, some of which are covered in this book.

The principles described in the text are often illustrated with practical examples and can be applied to most public sector, and not-for-profit services. Self-development questions are given at the end of each chapter to allow the reader to consider how the techniques discussed can be applied to specific service areas within their organisation.

This book is one of a series of “Essential Skills for the Public Sector” titles. The series aims to assist public sector managers become more efficient and effective in carrying out their important management responsibilities. We consider this book to be an important part of the tool kit for public sector management development.

Chapter 2

What is Quality?

Defining Quality

Quality is extremely important for the public sector and is a term that is used frequently with respect to public sector services. Quality is often used in the context of:

- *Establishing value for money*
- *Setting quality thresholds for service provision*
- *Creating an image*
- *Public perception*
- *Service specification*

Quality, by its very nature, is subjective and will mean different things to different people. It is also accepted that there are different levels of quality. Hence, defining quality in a general way is virtually impossible.

Despite the difficulties with definitions, there exist a number of standardised definitions of quality, some of which are given as follows:

"Quality is conformance to requirements"

Philip B Crosby - Quality is Free

"Quality is always relative to a set of requirements"
ISO 9000 principles

"Quality is the degree of excellence"
Concise Oxford English Dictionary

Many authors do not try to define quality, but treat quality as a concept which is interpreted by individuals and organisations with respect to different goods, services and objectives.

What is clear is that quality needs to be defined if it is to be understood in the same way by everybody. There are a variety of factors that influence the quality definition, and understanding these will help to ensure the most appropriate definition is developed for the organisation or service.

The types of factors which influence quality include:

a) The strategic objectives of the organisation with respect to service provision

b) The organisational value systems

c) Consumer attitudes and expectations

d) Employees attitudes and expectations

e) The market place

f) The communication methods being applied

These factors are explained further as follows:

Strategic objectives with respect to the provision of services

- *The key purpose of the service needs to be established:*
  - *Long lasting*
  - *Investment*
  - *Life enhancement*
  - *Re-cycling*
  - *Prevention*
  - *Cure*
  - *Protection*
  - *Value added*
  - *Enforcement*
  - *Customer satisfaction*
- *There may be one or a combination of different service objectives that need to be achieved*

Organisational value systems

- *Usually represented by policies on issues such as:*
  - *Equality*
  - *Customer care*
  - *Health and safety*
  - *Environment*
  - *Sustainability*
  - *Profitability*

- *Accountability*
- *Social/community responsibility*

- *The policies may in some cases conflict with one another leading to a confused value system*

Consumer attitudes and expectations

The consumers of products and services often make assumptions which may or may not be true, for example:

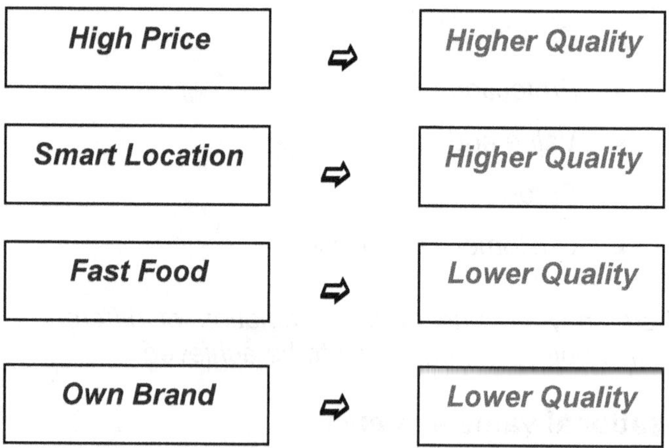

- *These assumptions may be influenced by a range of external factors such as:*
    - *Family/home environment*
    - *Friends/peers*
    - *Work environment*
    - *Public opinion*
    - *Past experience*

  - *Media*
  - *Image*

- *The consumer's perception of quality will be affected by their own attitude and expectation.*
- *In formulating the quality definition, the consumer's most common attitudes and expectations need to be taken into account.*

Employee Attitudes and Expectations

- *The quality definition, particularly in the public sector, may be strongly affected by employee's attitudes and expectations. It is they who deliver the service and interpret how the organisation's values are put into practice.*
- *This interpretation and implementation process is often determined by the employee's own set of influences, which are typically the same as those listed for the consumer.*

The Market Place

- *The nature of the market place affects the quality definition, in particular with respect to what is considered high and low quality.*
- *The market place may be characterised in a number of ways, including the following:*
  - *Monopoly (a single supplier)*
  - *Oligopoly (a few influential suppliers)*
  - *Cartel operations (suppliers acting in unison)*
  - *High number of suppliers*

- *Low number of suppliers*
- *High level of demand*
- *Low level of demand*
- *High cost of entry*
- *Low cost of entry*

For example, in the case of a market place where there are a high number of suppliers, the impact of strong competition will affect how quality is defined, i.e. suppliers will try to gain a competitive advantage by differentiating their products and services, often using quality criteria as the distinguishing feature.

Communication Methods Being Applied

- *Individuals have a variable understanding of quality depending on the messages that are communicated about the product or service, and the communication method used. These methods may be:*
    - *Written*
    - *Visual*
    - *Verbal*

using a range of techniques such as the internet, publicity literature, video, television, radio, word of mouth and so on

One of the key issues surrounding quality is whether or not it is understood by all the relevant parties concerned, such as:

- *The organisation enabling the service provision*

- *The organisation providing the service (may be the same as the above)*
- *The employees delivering the service*
- *The consumers of the service*

The understanding of the quality definition needs to be consistent amongst all the above parties to ensure "quality" means the same for everyone. Effective internal and external communication systems are important factors in achieving this.

The relationships and influences that help determine the quality definition are represented diagrammatically as follows:

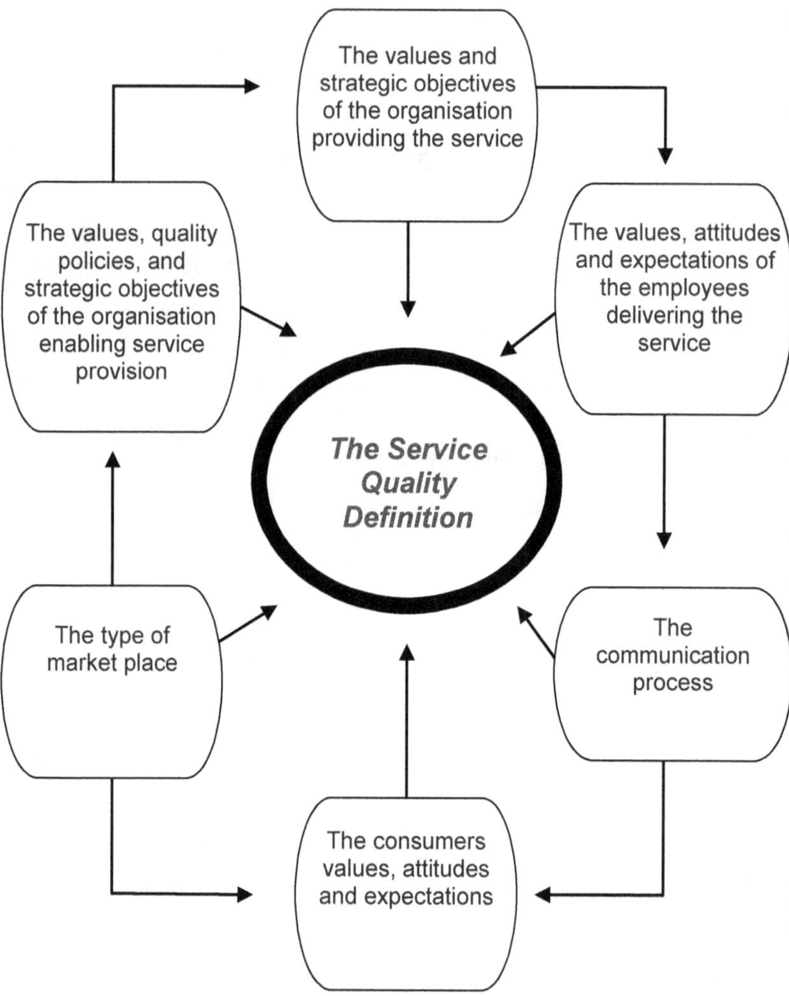
The values and strategic objectives of the organisation providing the service
The values, attitudes and expectations of the employees delivering the service
The communication process
The consumers values, attitudes and expectations
The type of market place
The values, quality policies, and strategic objectives of the organisation enabling service provision
The Service Quality Definition

An example of how all the parties should interact with respect to defining quality is shown as follows:

What is the quality definition for a school?

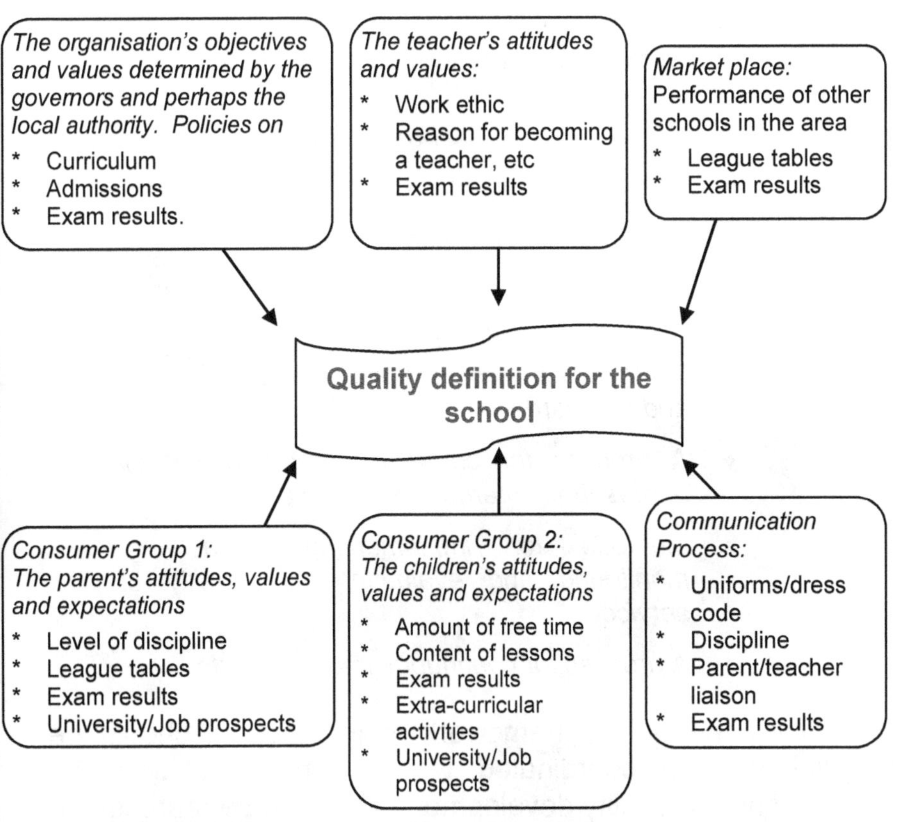

All perspectives in the above example show that exam results need to be an important part of the quality definition for this particular school.

Establishing a Quality Framework

In order to establish a quality environment, the organisation ideally needs to have a framework within which quality can be developed and maintained. As with most frameworks, quality should begin at the top of the organisation and be reflected in the overall goals and objectives.

The framework also needs to include:

- *Quality policies and procedures*
- *Methods for gaining customer/user feedback*
- *Methods for gaining employee feedback*
- *Methods for obtaining market information regarding quality*
- *A process for establishing quality definitions and standards*
- *A process for communication between all parties, both internal and external*
- *Methods for implementing, measuring, monitoring and evaluating the quality of service*
- *A process for continuous improvements*

When the quality framework is in place, it should be linked in a coordinated way to create a cycle for continuous quality development. This can be represented by the following diagram.

Cycle for continuous quality development

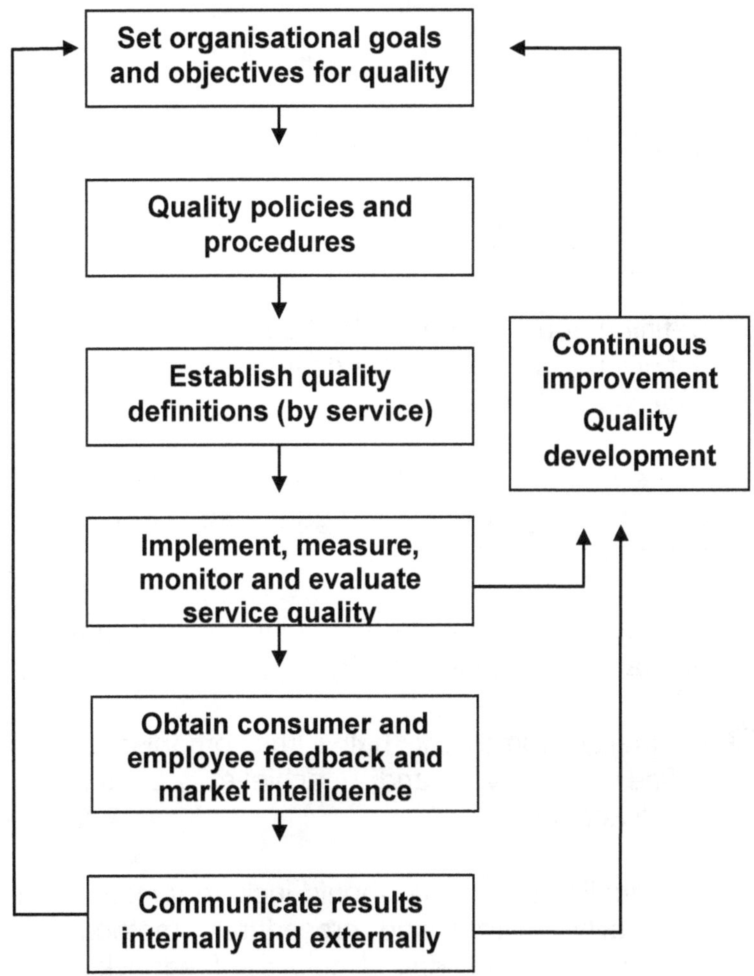

Summary

- ❑ Quality can be useful in helping public sector organisations achieve value for money, in setting quality thresholds for service provision and creating an image

- ❑ Defining quality can be difficult, therefore, a quality definition may need to be developed for individual services and products

- ❑ There are a number of factors involved in defining quality, which include the organisation's values, it's customers and employees

- ❑ The type of market place may influence the nature of quality levels delivered by suppliers

- ❑ A quality framework helps the organisation to define quality and achieve continuous improvement.

- ❑ The quality framework should include factors such as quality policies and procedures, methods of gaining customer and employee feedback, and market information with respect to quality

Exercise 1

Values and Objectives
~ Impact on Quality ~

For the following examples, set out what you consider to be:

a) **The most important values**

b) **The key strategic objectives**

c) **The impact on quality**

A person who purchases a Rolls Royce	***A person who purchases a small family car***
VALUES	*VALUES:*
OBJECTIVES:	*OBJECTIVES:*
IMPACT ON QUALITY:	*IMPACT ON QUALITY:*

Suggested solutions to this exercise can be found on page 122

Exercise 2

Service Quality Definitions

1. Identify below, the five most influential values to a local authority and the five most important values to a private business. What impact do these have on the way quality would be defined for the delivery of a school bus service?

Local Authority Values

1) ....

2) ....

3) ....

4) ....

5) ....

Quality Definition for School Bus Service

Private Sector Business Values

1) ....
2) ....
3) ....
4) ....
5) ....

Quality Definition for School Bus Service

Suggested solutions to this exercise can be found on page 123

Exercise 3

Service Quality Definitions

Consider one or more of your services, and identify with respect to each of the following categories, the factors which are taken into account when establishing service quality. *(see example given for "quality definition for a school" in this chapter)*

Objectives

Values

Consumer Attitude and Expectations

Employee Attitudes and Expectations

Market Place

Communication Methods

State a Quality Definition for your Service

Chapter 3

Setting Quality Standards

Purpose of Quality Standards

Having developed a quality definition, quality standards are then used to identify tangible benchmarks against which service delivery can be measured. For any given product or service this is a particularly important way of letting the public know what is meant by "quality". Within the public sector, quality standards are increasingly being published, and should provide the following:

- *A clear statement of what the consumer can expect from the service*
- *A clear statement of how employees are expected to perform with respect to service delivery*
- *A benchmark for monitoring the service and the extent to which quality standards are being met*
- *A basis for distinguishing the service quality from those of other providers*
- *A basis for evaluating services and assessing value for money*
- *A basis for the preparation of service specifications to be adhered to by internal and external service providers*

- *A basis for allocating resources*

Types of Quality Standards

Quality standards are usually developed at two levels:

Tangible:	*Based on a service specification where the service is broken down into detailed processes and functions, which can be documented with specific and tangible outcomes.*
Intangible:	*Based on relationship/interaction between provider and consumer, e.g. How helpful were staff? Was information given in a way that could be understood? etc.*

Tangible standards, such as response times, are easier to set than the intangible ones such as helpfulness and attitude.

Examples of quality standards established by a local authority housing department are shown in the following table.

Type of Service Activity	*Quality Standard*	*Tangible*	*Intangible*
Estate warden service	Ensure full tenant involvement and satisfaction		✓
Provide smoke alarms	To meet all regulatory standards	✓	
Establish a housing advice one stop shop	Provide impartial advice and information		✓
Major structural repairs to defective dwellings	To comply with current building regulations	✓	
Central repairs reporting	Respond to caller within 15 seconds	✓	
Void property repairs	To prepare properties for letting to a standard that achieves a letting on a first viewing	✓	

Some organisations identify different achievement levels within a quality standard allowing for:

The Ideal

(standards are fully met i.e. zero defect)

The Attainable

(standards are met within an acceptable range, e.g. 95% of the time)

The Minimum

(below which is an unacceptable level of quality; for many organisations this is usually the current level of service quality)

All organisations should be striving towards the ideal which means there is always scope for improvement (See cycle for continuous quality development, page 14).

In the private sector, service standards are often underwritten with generous promises to the consumer, e.g.

"30 days free trial and if not totally satisfied with the product your money back"

"If we are more than 20 minutes late with your pizza delivery you don't have to pay"

Some services, such as those delivered by certain professions, have standards set out in guidelines and ethical codes. Adherence to these standards is monitored by the relevant professional bodies.

Other standards are enforceable because they are underwritten by legislation, and if these standards are not met, the consumer may have a right to make a legal claim. This is particularly relevant to some public sector organisations which have a statutory duty to provide certain services.

Governments in many countries have established Citizen's Charters which underpin the principle of having public service standards which are defined, and hence can be expected by the public. This supports a customer-focused approach to public service delivery. It also requires organisation's to set relevant standards.

When considering quality standards, the ISO 9000 plain English definition includes the following:

> ***The quality of something can be determined by comparing a set of inherent characteristics with a set of requirements. If those inherent characteristics meet all requirements, high or excellent quality is achieved. If those characteristics do not meet all requirements, a low or poor level of quality is achieved. Quality is, therefore, a question of degree.***

According to this definition, *quality* is a relative concept.

Developing Standards for Public Sector Services

There is an increasing demand for public sector services to be of "high quality", and representing value for money. Once quality has been defined, the organisation has to translate it into documented standards that can be measured and monitored.

It may be very difficult to establish standards for certain types of public service. For example:

- *Services for which it is difficult to define quality in the first instance, e.g. prevention type services*

- *Services were the concept of quality differs greatly between the service provider and consumer, e.g. enforcement type services*
- *Services where quality is very subjective, e.g. caring type services*

If a structured approach is taken to developing standards, some of these difficulties can be overcome. One approach is to break down the service into its composite stages as follows:

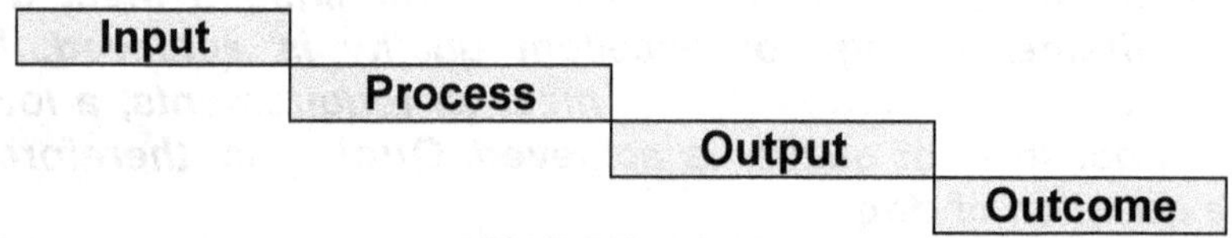

At each stage there will be varying degrees of interaction between the service provider, employees, and recipients of the service. It is through this interaction that quality standards can be developed. Depending on the nature of the service, developing standards will prove more difficult at some stages than at others. By separating the service into its composite stages, all aspects of the service will be taken into account, and not just those areas where standards are easy to develop.

Input, process, output and outcome standards are discussed as follows.

Input Standards

These relate to those elements required to deliver the service.

Inputs include:

- *Staffing resources*
- *Physical resources*
- *Financial resources*
- *Customer enquiries*

Quality standards can be developed around each of these, for example:

Input	***Standards***
Staff	*Qualifications, experience, attitude, service knowledge, etc.*
Facilities	*Accessibility, fitness for purpose, sufficiency, etc.*
Finance	*Level, accessibility, flexibility, etc.*
Enquiries	*Accuracy, completeness, clarity, relevance, responsiveness, etc.*

An example of possible input standards for a school is given as follows:

Teachers: *Set standards with respect to qualifications and experience in teaching each subject*

Pupils: *Set standards with respect to how pupils are allocated to the school and classes within the school. The nature of these standards will be determined by the ethos and objectives of the individual school, e.g. selection may be based on testing, locality, religious background, or any manner of combinations.*

School environment:	*Set standards with respect to school buildings, playing areas, class sizes, meals, and so on*
Finances:	*Set standards with respect to budgets, charges, collection, administration, and so on*

Process Standards

The process aspect of a service is "how" it is delivered. For some services the process is clearly documented and broken down into a number of steps, each of which can be standardised, monitored and controlled. Other services are very individual in nature and hence the process is different in every case, although there may be a commonality of approach to service delivery.

The starting point for setting standards with regard to the process is to identify the common features of the service.

> *For example, an advice centre will give different advice depending on the circumstances of each case, however, there may be a common approach to conducting a meeting; keeping records; validating advice given; and so on. Quality*

standards can be set around all of these areas. This does not necessarily guarantee the advice given was "quality advice", i.e. in line with the quality definition for the service. Whilst the quality of the advice may be very subjective, the output from the service may assist in determining the quality standard arising from the process. For example, collecting and collating data from the experience of the service users will provide indicators as to the perceived quality. Standards can be set around target levels for the user experience.

The quality of the process will be affected by the quality of the original input, hence the importance of ensuring that the input meets certain quality standards.

Output Standards

Unlike a product, the output from a service is not always tangible, and hence the standards for output may be difficult to devise. Output standards can be developed around the following areas.

Output	***Standards***
Tangible evidence, e.g. a report, a placement, a decision, a penalty, etc.	*Content, timing, accessibility, responsiveness, staff attitudes and behaviour, etc.*
Consumer satisfaction	*Consumer feedback, levels of satisfaction, levels of complaints, responsiveness, methods of communication, etc.*
Solution, resolution, prevention, etc.	*Timing, comparative results, safety, costs, etc.*

The following example considers how quality standards may be developed for outputs:

One of the outputs from the fire service is extinguishing a fire. This would be considered to be a "solution" output. The quality standards that could be developed for this would include the speed with which the fire was extinguished; the level of safety adopted; and the cost. Other standards such as customer satisfaction levels would also apply, but may not be as important to the overall quality definition, i.e. safety and speed may take priority.

Outcome Standards

Whilst outputs can lead to a wide range of possible outcomes, in some cases outcomes and outputs may be the same.

The eventual outcome from a service is often not seen immediately, and may take a long time to be realised. Hence, identifying outcomes may require considerable resources. These resources are not always available to the public sector, however, this does not mean quality standards cannot be set with respect to outcomes. In many cases, standards are most likely to be based on "expected" outcomes as opposed to "actual" outcomes. These expected outcomes are often based on research and may be general, as opposed to specific, for the individual service in question.

Some of the more common outcomes can be generalised into the following categories:

Outcome	***Standards***
Prevention/ Solution	*Reduction or elimination of incidents (crime, sickness, accidents, etc.)*
Quality of life	*Health, education, wealth, employment, social behaviour, etc.*
Environment	*Cleanliness, health, safety, conservation, image, etc.*
Consumer satisfaction	*Long term shift in attitudes, changes in consumer behaviour, consumer education, etc.*

An example is given as follows:

> *When children services make a decision to place a child in foster care, or for adoption, the expected outcome will be to enhance the child's quality of life. Standards can be set as to the incremental benefits that should be gained with respect to some of the quality of life benchmarks.*

It is clear from the above that considerable work is required if appropriate standards are to be developed for all services at all levels, and this will take time and resources.

The quality definition is fundamental to the process of setting standards, and an organisation may have to revert to this stage before being able to develop a range of standards that are relevant and meaningful.

Summary

- Quality standards provide a benchmark for measuring the quality of service provision
- Quality standards should be published so that consumers and staff know what they are
- Quality standards may be tangible and intangible. Tangible ones are easier to set
- Services should be broken down to reflect input, process and output requirements and expected outcomes. Standards should be set in all areas
- Some services may be input driven, particularly where outputs and outcomes are difficult to define
- The quality definition is fundamental to developing appropriate quality standards

Exercise 4

Quality Standards

Insert your public sector definition for the School Bus Service from Exercise 2, then set a number of tangible and intangible quality standards that you would be prepared to put on show to the general public.

QUALITY DEFINITION

QUALITY STANDARDS

Tangible

Intangible

Suggested solutions to this exercise can be found on page 125

Exercise 5

Quality Standards

PART (A)

List the current quality standards that have been developed for your service area and analyse them in the following way. (If you have none, go on to part B).

Standard	***Tangible***	***Intangible***	***Input***	***Process***	***Output***	***Outcome***
e.g.						
we respond to an enquiry within 5 working days of receipt	☑	☐	☐	☑	☑	☐
	☐	☐	☐	☐	☐	☐
	☐	☐	☐	☐	☐	☐
	☐	☐	☐	☐	☐	☐
	☐	☐	☐	☐	☐	☐
	☐	☐	☐	☐	☐	☐
	☐	☐	☐	☐	☐	☐

(Answers will vary according to the nature and the quality definition of your service)

PART (B)

Where there are gaps in the current range of standards, consider the new standards that need to be put in place; e.g. there may be output standards but no input ones or vice versa.

Standard	***Tangible***	***Intangible***	***Input***	***Process***	***Output***	***Outcome***
e.g.						
respond to an enquiry within 3 working days of receipt	☑	☐	☐	☑	☑	☐
	☐	☐	☐	☐	☐	☐
	☐	☐	☐	☐	☐	☐
	☐	☐	☐	☐	☐	☐
	☐	☐	☐	☐	☐	☐
	☐	☐	☐	☐	☐	☐
	☐	☐	☐	☐	☐	☐

PART (C)

For the new standards identified in part B, list the potential difficulties in setting and implementing them and how you consider those difficulties may be overcome.

Difficulties in Setting the Standards	***Possible Solutions***
e.g. insufficient staffing to respond within 3 days	e.g. review process for responding to enquiries for efficiencies

Chapter 4

Measuring and Monitoring Quality

Performance Indicators

Having established quality standards for a service, it is in the interest of the organisation, staff and consumers, to identify how actual service delivery measures up to those standards. To achieve this, the organisation/service provider should identify the most appropriate indicators of quality given the standards that have been set. These performance indicators can then be used as part of the performance measurement process. With consistent measurement over time, organisations can make a judgement as to the level of actual quality being achieved.

In chapter 3, quality standards were divided into two main categories, tangible and intangible. Performance indicators need to be developed for both types of standard so as to provide tangible evidence for measurement. When appropriate performance indicators have been identified, they can be used as a basis for setting performance targets. These targets may allow for some element of non-performance, particularly for services where it may not be possible to achieve 100% success, all of the time.

Whilst a wide range of suitable performance indicators can be developed for some services, a practical approach needs to be taken to identify the indicators that are most important with respect to the desired level of quality. This selection can be achieved by obtaining a consensus between provider and consumer as to what aspects of the service are the most important when determining the quality definition.

Performance indicators tend to fall into two categories:

Quantitative indicators provide data which is measurable and objective in nature, e.g. cost per hour, time taken, waste levels, etc.

Qualitative indicators provide data which is generally subjective in nature and more difficult to measure, e.g. customer opinions, staff attitudes, etc.

Most services will attract both types of indicator

In order to identify relevant performance indicators, the following questions should be answered:

Are any of the inputs critical to the service quality standard?

Are there any processes critical to the service quality standard?

What are the outputs that reflect the quality standards?

What outcome is expected from the service?

Is there scope to improve the service quality and redefine the standard?

An example is given as follows:

Service:	*Meals on wheels*
Quality Definition:	*To provide a caring delivery service of tasty, nutritious hot meals, to all eligible clients between 12.00pm and 1.00pm daily*
Extract from published Quality Standards:	• *Meals will be delivered within 10 minutes of the agreed time* • *Meals will be varied each day with high nutritional value, and be hot on arrival at client's premises* • *Staff will be courteous and helpful at all times*

Performance Indicators	**Quantitative**	**Qualitative**
Time of delivery to client	✓	
Range of menus offered each day	✓	✓
Temperature of meals on arrival	✓	
Number of meals provided each day	✓	
Nutritional value of ingredients	✓	✓
Method of food preparation	✓	✓
Staff qualifications	✓	✓
Method of delivery	✓	✓
Level of staff training	✓	✓
Friendliness of staff		✓
Time spent at the client's premises	✓	✓
Customer satisfaction	✓	✓

It should be noted that many of the performance indicators identified in the above example can be both quantitative and qualitative.

Having identified the performance indicators, the next stage is to develop sensible methods of measuring the indicators which are not too time consuming or bureaucratic.

Measuring Performance

Having identified a range of indicators as either quantitative, qualitative or both, the measurement of those indicators can be approached in the same way. Although there are often different ways of measuring the same indicator, the important factor to remember is that measurement should be practical. It should not result in the need for significant additional resources, otherwise this becomes an "additional" cost of quality.

Using the performance indicators identified in the previous *meals on wheels* example, the following quantitative and qualitative performance measures can be identified.

Performance Indicator	Performance Measure (Quantitative)	Performance Measure (Qualitative)
Time of delivery to client	Log of arrival time at each client	
Range of menus offered each day	Number of different menus offered each day	Content of each menu offered
Temperature of meals on arrival	Temperature readings on arrival at clients premises Temperature of containers used by provider	
Number of meals provided each day	Count of number of meals packaged for delivery Count of number of meals delivered	

Performance Indicator	Performance Measure (Quantitative)	Performance Measure (Qualitative)
Nutritional value of ingredients	Percentage of menu that includes "fresh" produce Salt, fat, and calorie content	Inspection of site during preparation and observation of "fresh" produce use
Method of food production	Audit of quality system in place for food production, logging number of exceptions to the system	Observation of methods used and general assessment of key indicators such as cleanliness, health and safety, etc.
Qualifications/ experience of staff	CVs of staff engaged in the service	Observing staff ability to perform certain functions
Method of delivery	Audit of delivery system and logging number of exceptions	Inspection of modes of transport used during delivery and general assessment of key indicators such as fitness for purpose, presentation of vehicle, etc.
Level of staff training	Detailed staff training records, identifying number of days training undertaken per person per annum	Details of range and content of training courses undertaken
Friendliness of staff		Client opinions gained from client surveys Staff opinions gained from staff surveys Observation and general assessment of staff performance on site
Time spent at the client's premises	Log of arrival time and departure time from each client	Client opinion of customer care gained from client surveys

Performance Indicator	Performance Measure (Quantitative)	Performance Measure (Qualitative)
Customer satisfaction	Customer satisfaction survey results for tangible indicators, e.g. was food hot?	Customer satisfaction survey for intangible indicators such as whether staff were helpful, caring, etc.

For each of these measures, targets should be set which act as a benchmark. For example:

- ❑ *Specify number of menu choices that should be on offer*
- ❑ *Specify number of meals that should be produced daily*
- ❑ *Specify the temperature range of the food*
- ❑ *Specify the level of non-conformance allowed when quality systems audited*
- ❑ *Specify the level of customer satisfaction expected*

The purpose of undertaking measurement is to ensure targets for performance are being met and quality standards are being maintained. Where organisations fail to meet targets, the reasons for failure should be investigated. Depending on the reasons identified for failing to meet standards, (such as changed conditions, unforeseen problems, and so on), it may be necessary to redefine the quality standards.

Performance measurement is therefore important for the following reasons, it:

- *Identifies whether or not quality standards are being met*
- *Identifies changes that need to be made to the service in order to meet quality standards (where possible)*
- *Identifies whether or not quality standards need to be revised (upwards or downwards)*
- *Provides a tangible method of identifying under performance, which in the case of a client/contractor relationship, may be the basis for penalties*
- *Provides the public with information on the standard of service being provided*

Monitoring Techniques

In order to monitor quality standards, efficient and effective data collection systems need to be in place. This data will provide information which will indicate whether or not performance targets have been met. Performance monitoring should be undertaken on a regular basis.

If the organisation has a policy and culture of continuous improvement, the results of monitoring should feed into service developments and new quality standards. Some organisations find continuous improvement difficult to achieve in practice, as there is often increasing service demand and diminishing resources. Even in these instances, performance monitoring has a value in highlighting the impact of reducing resources, and helping to identify ways in which standards can be maintained and targets met within a climate of cuts and savings.

Performance can be monitored at a number of levels within any organisation:

Corporate Level	
Monitoring	**Method**
• *Monitoring the achievement of strategic objectives as set out in the business plan, comparing what is actually happening with what is set out in the plan, and identifying why variances have occurred.* • *Reviewing organisational monitoring information on a regular basis such as key statistics on performance indicators, customer satisfaction ratings, etc.*	• *Regular business plan review meetings* • *Regular revision of business plan, adjustments to objectives and strategies, and communication of reviews and revisions* • *Regular assessment of values and quality policies* • *Regular consideration of value for money and the cost of quality*

Operational Level

Monitoring	Method
• *Monitoring the delivery of services, ensuring that standards are being maintained by collecting data and measuring actual performance against the standard* • *Identifying variances from set standards, areas of non-compliance, and satisfaction levels*	• *Analysing data collected from the measurement of performance indicators* • *Identifying areas where performance is not meeting set standards* • *Identifying areas for improvement and setting out appropriate action plans* • *Undertaking regular system audits to ensure information is accurate and complete* • *Undertaking regular satisfaction surveys*

Individual Level

Monitoring	Method
• *Monitoring individual performance against planned targets*	• *Setting targets at appraisal meetings* • *Reviewing targets at regular management meetings* • *Identifying areas where targets are not being met, and dealing with the reasons for non-performance* • *Setting individual action plans and monitoring their fulfilment*

In order to assist in performance monitoring, clear goals, objectives and targets should be set and backed up with action plans which identify what needs to be done, by whom, and by when.

Responsibility for performance monitoring is held at all levels within the organisation:

Directors	~	**Corporate level**
Managers	~	**Operational level, services and resource management**
All staff	~	**Individual level, self-monitoring, attitude, work ethic, etc.**

The achievement and monitoring of quality standards is dependent on how well standards are initially set, and the quality systems in place that allow sufficient and appropriate data to be collected so as to measure performance. Standards need to be constantly reviewed, and performance measures should become increasingly sophisticated such that the organisation, management, and all staff, adopt the values of a quality culture.

Summary

- Having established quality standards, it is in the interest of the organisation, staff and consumers to measure how the actual service delivery meets the standards

- Performance indicators need to be developed for tangible and intangible standards

- When performance indicators have been developed, they can be used as a basis for setting performance targets

- Performance indicators tend to fall into two categories: quantitative and qualitative

- Most services will attract both quantitative and qualitative indicators, however, it is far easier to measure quantitative indicators than qualitative ones

- Undertaking performance measurement ensures targets are being met and quality standards maintained

- Where organisations fail to meet the targets, reasons for failure should be investigated

Summary Continued

- Depending on the reasons for failing to meet standards, it may be necessary to redefine the quality standard to take account of changes in conditions, unforeseen problems, and so on

- In order to monitor quality standards successfully, there needs to be an efficient and effective data collection system

- To assist in the monitoring of performance, clear goals, objectives and targets need to be set and backed up with actions plans which identify what needs to be done, by whom, and by when

- Responsibility for performance monitoring is held at all levels within the organisation

- Standards need to be constantly reviewed, and performance measures need to become increasingly sophisticated, such that the organisation, the management and all staff adopt the values of a quality culture

Exercise 6

Performance Indicators

For each standard identified in Exercise 4, list at least two performance indicators (think about how they might be measured).

Standard	Performance Indicators

Standard	Performance Indicators

Suggested solutions to this exercise can be found on page 127

Exercise 7

Measuring Performance

Given the following 3 scenarios, answer the questions (a), (b) and (c) at the end of the exercise, for each case:

Case 1

The finance department produces financial control reports on a monthly basis which give managers information about the budget and actual spending in their departments. One of their quality standards is that these reports should be delivered within two weeks of the month end, and another is that they will process corrections within one month. On the whole, they have managed to achieve both of these quality standards. However, managers are concerned that the information is usually incorrect and out of date and therefore of little use, many managers often only file the reports. Some managers are considering setting up their own reports in order to obtain better information.

Case 2

The street cleansing service is supposed to sweep every footpath and empty bins on those footpaths once per week as per the specification in the contract. Their performance standard is that all rubbish and debris is removed from the footpath and all rubbish is removed from the bins and surrounding area after they have been emptied and swept. The contractor performs it's duty as per the specification.

Case 3

The front of house reception has recently undergone major restructuring with a view to introducing a quality service. The authority has described a quality reception service as "A reception where all people are treated with dignity and respect in a prompt and efficient manner." The quality standards for reception have been stated and displayed as follows:

- All enquiries at the front desk will be responded to within five minutes
- No one will be kept waiting in reception for more than ten minutes without being referred on to the appropriate service, e.g. cashiers, planning, etc.
- Receptionists will give out accurate information to all enquiries and provide practical assistance wherever possible
- Receptionists will maintain several information systems including visitors books, databases, enquiry logs, distribution of information records and service utilization records

There are four receptionists who are supposed to work together as a team on a shift basis, such that two people are present at all times. One of the receptionists has raised several issues with the manager:

- Not all receptionists can use the computer, therefore, most of the inputting is left to one person, whilst the others are not always using the computer to obtain the most up to date information
- Although waiting times have been adhered to, quite often, the departments who are supposed to deal with the enquirer do not respond promptly, so customers are ushered into interview rooms (not waiting in reception) to wait for quite a long time

- Some receptionists are not very helpful and redirect enquiries that they could have dealt with immediately at the reception desk

The manager responsible for reception feels that things are going well as there have not been any complaints as yet (there used to be at least 3 per week), and the management information systems seem to be kept up to date and identify that enquiries are being dealt with in a proper manner.

a) Is this a quality service?

Case 1

Case 2

Case 3

b) What type of performance measurement would you undertake?

Case 1

Case 2

Case 3

c) How could the service be improved?

Case 1

Case 2

Case 3

Suggested solutions to this exercise can be found on page 130

Exercise 8

Measuring Performance

Given the quality standards for your own service, set out the ways in which you currently measure performance against the standard. Think about other ways in which performance measurement and monitoring could be undertaken.

Type of Service: ____________			
Service Standard	**Performance Indicators**	**Measurement Methods**	**New Ways of Measurement**

Chapter 5

Quality Management

Total Quality Management

To operate an effective quality management process, the whole organisation has to be involved in total quality management. This requires quality systems which cover the whole range of activities from inputs to outcomes. Total quality management needs to operate at a number of levels as shown below.

Strategic Level

Focus on:

- *achieving long term objectives*
- *establishing the overarching mission to which everyone works*
- *developing the corporate image*
- *survival of the organisation*

Owned by senior management

Operational Level

Focus on:

- *standard processes and procedures*
- *team working*
- *increasing productivity*
- *reducing waste and errors*
- *achieving consistency*

Owned by managers and the workforce

Customer Level

Focus on:

- *meeting customer requirements*
- *establishing customer perceptions*
- *anticipating future customer needs*
- *changing to meet external demands*
- *achieving customer satisfaction*

Owned by marketing departments and some front-line staff

Development Level

Focus on:

- *staff development*
- *staff training*
- *staff participation*
- *individual responsibility*
- *individual performance*

Owned by personnel departments and some managers

A truly quality focussed organisation, requires all its members to feel part of, and own, all levels of a total quality management system. To achieve this, the following types of underpinning processes should be in place:

- *Business planning cycles*
- *Performance management systems*
- *Appraisal systems*
- *Quality circles*
- *Codes of practice*
- *Quality manuals*
- *Consumer liaison*

These processes are discussed further in the following paragraphs.

Business Planning Cycles

Quality is dependent upon the organisational objectives and these are developed as part of the business planning process. Business planning is therefore a fundamental underpinning process which is essential if the organisation is to become truly quality orientated. The business plan will have objectives around products, services, marketing and so on, all of which will have a quality dimension. The business plan will identify targets and strategies which will enable objectives to be achieved.

Business plans should be developed on a regular basis as part of a routine, and where possible, all parts of the organisation should be involved. The business planning cycle is an on-going process which enables continual review and evaluation of objectives, taking account of internal and external factors.

Performance Management Systems

The concept of performance management advocates that all staff have specific targets to work towards, and are managed in a way which encourages them to be innovative. In so doing, staff are not only encouraged to meet their targets, but to exceed them. Performance management allows managers to give credit to those staff who have performed successfully. Quality should be built into staff performance targets and be regularly monitored and reviewed, e.g. daily, weekly or monthly. Some organisations may incorporate performance management as part of their overall appraisal system.

Appraisal Systems

The appraisal system is fundamental to the quality organisation and most of the recognised quality kite marks expect organisations to have an effective appraisal system in place. It is important that the appraisal system has the following features:

- it links the individual's targets to the organisations' objectives
- it involves interaction between the appraiser and appraisee
- the appraiser is trained on how to conduct an appraisal
- there is consistency across the organisation as to how the appraisal is undertaken and the results used
- appraisals occur at least once per year
- the appraisals cover all aspects of the individual's work including subjective areas such as attitudes
- the appraisee understands how he/she is performing and what needs to be done in the case of under performance
- the appraisal sets targets for future periods

- the appraisal identifies future training needs which are fed into the training plans for the individual and the organisation

In addition to the above, some appraisals have scoring systems which may link into reward systems or be used as a basis for recommending promotions.

The appraisal can be a powerful tool with respect to ensuring staff understand and implement the quality standards within the organisation.

Quality Circles

A quality circle is a form of working group whereby a number of staff come together in order to improve the quality of their product or service. This is one of a variety of techniques that involves the workforce in maintaining and developing quality within the organisation.

The quality circle will include a group of staff led by a supervisor, not too large (up to 10) who are performing the same or similar work.

The Quality Circle should:

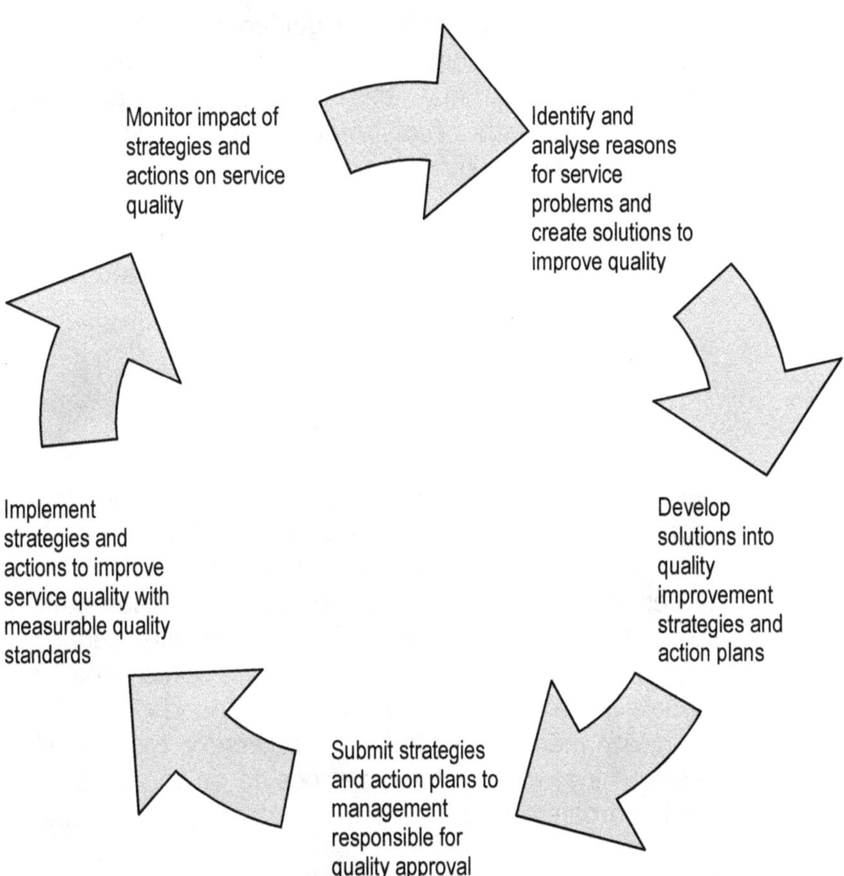

Ultimately, the quality circle should become sufficiently trusted within an organisation allowing management decision making to be devolved to lower levels. This will enable the process to move more quickly by eliminating unnecessary bureaucracy. Quality circles only tend to work in organisations which are quality centred, and where many of the other underpinning quality processes are in place.

Codes of Practice

These codes provide staff with guidance as to how to deliver service, including aspects which are linked to quality. The codes may be internal or provided by external bodies with a monitoring role (particularly true of professions). A quality organisation will ensure all such codes are strictly enforced. Breaches of the code may result in staff being disciplined and, depending on the nature of breach, losing their professional status.

Quality Manuals

These are usually internally developed by the organisation and identify the quality standard for each aspect of service. Ideally the manual will break down the service into its component parts and provide staff with a clear understanding of how a quality service should be produced and delivered. Some quality manuals are so large they are not user friendly. Ideally, the quality manual should be an accessible tool for all staff, and increasingly they are located on the intranet of many organisations.

In order to develop a practical quality manual, the following issues should be considered:

- *The quality principles underlying the organisation and its approach to service delivery*
- *Development of a clear service specification, i.e. services should be clearly defined along with quantitative and qualitative quality standards*
- *Breaking the service down into its component elements/ stages*

- *Identifying the input, process, output, and outcome of each stage*
- *The quality performance indicators that will be measured and monitored in order to ensure quality standards are achieved*
- *How the service can be audited to ensure procedures set out in the manual are being adhered to*
- *Staff involvement in all aspects of the above*

Quality manuals benefit from the use of flow charts which are simple to understand and user friendly. Developing flow charts often assist staff to consider exactly how the service is delivered, and can result in changes and enhancements which then lead to quality improvements.

Consumer Liaison

As the majority of public sector organisations are service based, it is important that they have an effective method of communicating with users/consumers. This is the group which often determines acceptable quality standards. A quality organisation should establish a consumer liaison process which allows for feedback on existing services and suggestions for potential new service developments. This can be achieved by implementing some of the following:

- *frequent consumer surveys*
- *focus groups*

- *consumer consultation on change and developments*
- *consumer participation (e.g. representation on boards of management, committees, working parties, and so on)*
- *internet networking sites*
- *internet blogs on service*
- *suggestion boxes*
- *feedback sheets*
- *public meetings*
- *open days*
- *newsletters*
- *complaints procedures*

Quality Audits

The audit is a fundamental part of quality control and therefore an essential process for a quality organisation. The audit of quality systems highlight the extent and frequency with which quality standards are being met. For example, 90% of the service meets the standard 85% of the time.

Where the service has undergone the process of establishing a quality definition, quality standards, performance indicators, measurement processes and continual monitoring, the quality audit should be relatively straightforward.

It is common for quality audits to be undertaken internally with an officer having responsibility for the audit. This may be a specialist post, or there may be a specialist department responsible for quality. Another approach is to make responsibility for quality audits part of the managers' overall responsibilities. Ideally, those responsible for quality audits should:

- *have a clear understanding of what the organisation wishes to achieve from the audit*
- *be independent of the service being delivered (i.e. not part of the delivery team)*
- *have no vested interest in the outcome of the audit*
- *have relevant service knowledge (i.e. knows what to look out for)*
- *have sufficient standing in the organisation to ensure recommendations are implemented*

These criteria favour the "independent auditor" as opposed to the manger. However, there are benefits in having someone close to the service, such as the manager, undertaking regular audits. These include:

- *detailed service knowledge*
- *understanding the problems that may be the cause of poor performance and non-achievement of standards*
- *speed of corrective action (no need to wait for an external report)*
- *ownership of the quality system*
- *responsibility and accountability for meeting quality standards*

Audits can sometimes be viewed as intrusive, with staff regarding the process with suspicion, and a way of checking they are performing their jobs properly. Further, audits are typically associated with the monitoring of the organisation's finances and financial systems, sometimes with the emphasis on detecting fraud and irregularities.

The purpose of the audit should be fully explained and seek to:

- ❖ *establish what standards are being achieved and how often*
- ❖ *identify areas where quality standards are falling short of the acceptable levels*
- ❖ *ensure the measurement and monitoring processes are being implemented*
- ❖ *suggest new ways to measure and monitor quality where the existing ones are proving inadequate*
- ❖ *provide recommendations for improvements to all aspects of service delivery including the quality of input, process, output and outcome.*
- ❖ *produce a written report which can be reviewed, and progress monitored at subsequent audits*

The audit therefore benefits the whole organisation.

In some cases external organisations are engaged to audit quality systems. These may be quality consultancies, or professional bodies which monitor the standards required to gain and maintain membership of their profession. Where an organisation has achieved a quality kite mark of some kind such as ISO 9000, the awarding body undertakes a regular assessment, similar to an audit, to ensure standards are being maintained.

Summary

- Total quality management needs to operate at the following levels:

  Strategic
  Operational
  Customer
  Development

- Ideally all members of the organisation should feel part of, and own, all levels of total quality management

- In order to develop and maintain a quality organisation, there needs to be underpinning processes such as business planning cycles, performance management systems, appraisal systems, quality circles, codes of practice, quality manuals and consumer liaison processes

- In order for a performance management system to play an effective role in establishing a quality organisation, it has to be implemented at all levels and monitored on a regular basis

- Quality systems need to be regularly audited

- Audits can be undertaken by internal or external experts. Ideally, the auditor should be totally independent of the service

Exercise 9

Total Quality Management in Practice

A prison service provider (APS), recently took management of a prison having been successful in a tendering process. The prison has the following problems:

- *very poor staff relations*
- *a reputation for regular disturbances*
- *poor working conditions*
- *dull and dirty common areas*
- *provision of a very limited range of activities (partly due to lack of appropriate staffing)*
- *poor standards of catering (meals low on variety and nutrition)*
- *very bad image with local residents and prison visitors*

The new contract manager decided the best way forward would be to look at the whole organisation, and implement a total quality management approach to all aspects of prison life.

The time scale for implementation was one year, as after this time APS would have its first performance assessment. The key performance targets included:

- *decrease in staff turnover*
- *reduction in number of disturbances*

- *reduction in number of complaints*
- *refurbishment of common areas*
- *increased number of activities*

APS won the tender based on a 10% saving on historical costs and therefore performance targets have to be achieved within a lower budget than had previously been spent on the prison; any new changes will have to be very low cost in order to stay within budget.

The manager needs to develop a list of actions setting out all the things she wishes to do in order to start developing a total quality management system.

Given the above, identify a list of actions covering all aspects of the organisation which you consider the manager should undertake.

1 ____________________________________

2 ____________________________________

3 ____________________________________

4 ____________________________________

5 ____________________________________

6 ____________________________________

7 ____________________________________

8 ____________________________________

9 ____________________________________

10 ____________________________________

Suggested solutions to this exercise can be found on page 132

Exercise 10

TQM Systems

Describe how you would implement TQM in your area of service

List the implementation stages:

What problems may you encounter in trying to operate a TQM system?

Chapter 6

Investing in Quality

Cost of Quality

It is often assumed that increasing service quality requires an increase in cost. Hence, many people associate a more expensive service with higher quality. These two assumptions are in many cases untrue. The relationship between quality and cost can be wide and varied depending on the nature of the service or product being delivered.

The following diagrams illustrate a number of relationships between cost and quality

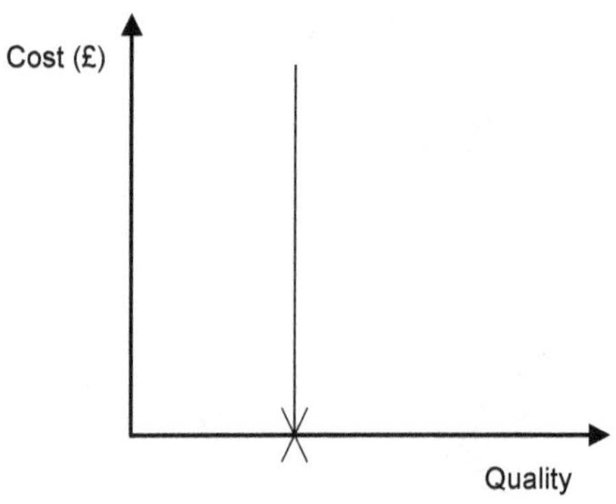

Same quality regardless of cost

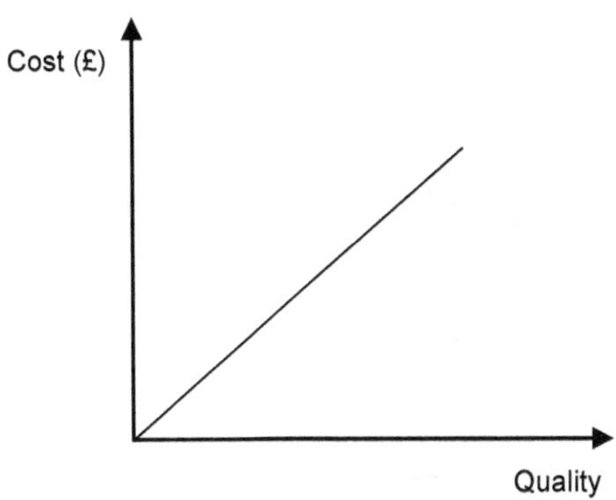

Higher costs lead to higher quality

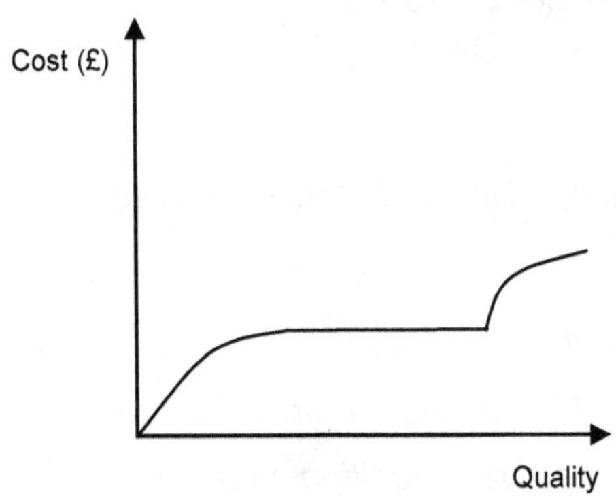

Quality increases initially with cost until a certain point, whereby quality continues to increase without additional cost. After a while further quality improvements require further investment. This is a typical profile

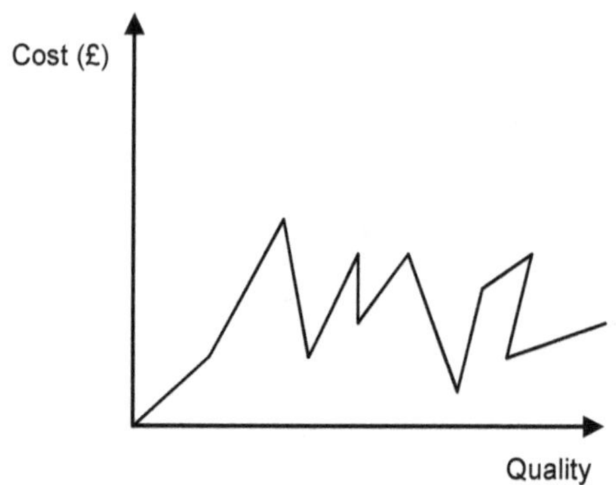

No consistent relationship between quality and cost

In order to determine the quality/cost relationship for a service, the organisation needs to establish its definition of "quality" and of "cost". Defining quality has been discussed in chapter 2.

The cost of quality for a specific service, should take into account the following:

- *what key factors enhance service quality?*
- *what inputs are required to implement those factors?*
- *do the inputs represent a direct additional cost, if so, how much?*
- *what are the differences in outputs and outcomes as a result of the enhancement to quality and can these be measured in tangible terms?*

When assessing the cost of quality it is necessary to take account of all costs such as:

- *those costs directly attributable to quality enhancement, e.g. the cost of an additional member of staff providing additional service, the cost of training, the cost of refurbishment, and so on*
- *those costs indirectly resulting from increasing the level of quality, e.g. increased service demand*

An example of how the cost and quality relationship can be assessed is given as follows:

A local authority had very poor satisfaction ratings for its advice centre and decided to increase the quality of service. The quality definition for the service being:

> "a fast response to the public's enquiries giving accurate and complete information which meets their requirements"

The quality improvements would include:

	Cost (£)	
Enhancing the computer system to increase the speed of response, and extending the database to provide more complete and up to date information	15,000	*
All staff to receive training on the enhanced system, customer care and dealing with enquiries	10,000	*
Employing an additional staff member to attend to enquirers and reduce waiting times	10,000	

Refurbishment of the offices, including comfortable seating for those who are waiting	5,000	*
Introduction of a ticket queuing system which allows enquirers to know how long their wait is likely to be	3,000	*
Sub-total	43,000	
Other costs *(comprising mainly of increased management time spent monitoring the use of the new systems and the performance of staff)*	7,000	
TOTAL COSTS	**50,000**	

** one off costs*

The success of the quality initiative will be measured by the change in customer satisfaction ratings, decreasing complaints, along with the quantity and quality of the output from the advice centre.

The quality of a service can sometimes be improved with relatively minor changes. For example, the way in which staff provide information, that is with a pleasant manner; a smile; empathy; sympathy; etc. This type of quality enhancement may cost nothing in financial terms, but still yield increases in customer satisfaction ratings and decreased complaints.

In the private sector, the cost of quality is sometimes measured in terms of the cost of non-performance and poor quality. This is calculated by considering:

- *the level of penalties incurred (if the service is under contract)*

- *the amount of compensation that needs to be paid (in the event that the service provider has been negligent)*
- *the amount of insurance to be paid (this often increases in line with increased claims arising from poor service)*
- *the amount of returns received (in the case of products not being fit for the purpose)*
- *the amount of lost custom (resulting from very low satisfaction with the goods or services being provided)*

The above approach is also relevant for the public sector.

The fact that poor quality has a cost means that investing in quality enhancement can produce a saving.

The cost of poor quality service in the public sector is highlighted as follows:

- *increased complaints requiring implementation of the complaints procedures, which uses additional staff time.*
- *low morale leading to high staff turnover, lost experience and greater need for training new staff*
- *correcting errors, e.g. resending tax demands due to incorrect tax calculations*
- *generating further enquiries as customers are not satisfied with the initial responses to their questions, e.g. lack of informed help line staff*

- *increased legal costs arising from poor services leading to breaches of statutory responsibilities, e.g. some social services cases where poor service delivery has led to legal action*

- *wasted resources as facilities/services under-utilised, e.g. local authority properties left empty due to their condition*

Benefits of Quality

If there is to be an investment in quality, then there has to be some benefits arising from the investment. Benefits can be looked at in two ways:

Tangible Benefits

- Increased service output
- Increased satisfaction levels
- Reductions in complaints
- Improved working conditions
- Reduced errors/waste

Intangible Benefits

- Reduced stress levels
- Reduced sickness
- Improved staff relations
- Improved customer relations
- Improved public image

In order to compare the benefits with the costs, an organisation needs to be able to translate these benefits into monetary terms. This can prove to be a difficult task, particularly with respect to intangible benefits. So that this translation can be achieved, there is a need to maintain records with respect to the areas where benefits are expected. These can be very specific, for example sickness rates, output volumes, numbers of complaints and so on. Monetary savings can be calculated for these types of benefits in a relatively straight forward manner.

Other areas are more difficult, such as image. An example of translating image into monetary terms, is where the image of the public service is so good, users are prepared to pay for it, or pay more. These increased revenues can be attributed to the level of quality. For example, upgraded leisure centre facilities could result in increased charges being acceptable to the public.

Using the example in the previous section which demonstrated the cost of quality for the advice centre, the benefits of quality could be identified as follows:

In the first year:

	Benefit (£)
Increased satisfaction resulting in less complaints needing to be investigated *(saving in staff time)*	5,000
Increased satisfaction resulting in faster processing time as users are more relaxed, non-aggressive, etc. *(saving in staff time)*	10,000
Reduced waiting times resulting in a reduction of space needed for queuing *(saving in office space and overheads)*	3,000
Provision of more accurate and complete information provided, reducing the need for follow-up enquiries *(saving in staff time)*	10,000
Reduced staff sickness rates *(saving in time lost due to absence, overtime payments and use of agency staff)*	5,000
Total Benefit	**33,000 per annum**

In order to arrive at the above figures, it is necessary to have undertaken costing exercises such as the cost per hour of staff and management, and the cost per unit of service such as answering an enquiry. With the unit cost information, it is possible to identify in monetary terms, the savings resulting from increased quality.

Cost Benefit Analysis

Given that there is a cost to quality and an expected benefit, it should be possible to make an assessment as to whether the investment in quality is worthwhile. This is generally the case if the benefits can be shown to outweigh the costs.

Continuing to use the previous advice centre example:

> ***The cost of the quality enhancements to the advice centre, can be broken down between one off costs and annual costs as follows:***

	Cost (£)
One off costs	33,000
Annual costs	17,000
Total Cost	50,000

> The annual benefits are £33,000 (see previous page), therefore, the net annual benefit after deduction of the annual costs above are £16,000 (£33,000 – £17,000).
>
> A cost benefit analysis calculation would show the net annual benefits will cover the one off investment cost in just over 2 years (2 x £16,000). After this point the benefits arising from a higher quality service will outweigh the cost of implementation.

There are other factors to consider when undertaking a cost benefit analysis exercise. These include:

- *availability of resources/resource limitations*
- *alternative uses for resources*

- *the cost/implications of not improving quality*
- *acceptable payback period (some organisations require immediate net benefits)*
- *organisation's commitment to quality*

Quality and Value for Money

In the private sector, quality levels are balanced with demand for the product, and the price that the consumer will bear. Therefore, quality enhancements can often be passed on to the consumer through the price. In the public sector the relationship is not so clear cut and often quality has to be balanced with value for money. This is especially important in the current climate of reductions to public spending and user demand for high quality services which cannot always be reconciled; for example, some service quality may be lost in order to meet increased demand within limited resources.

Where public sector services are being outsourced, quality standards can be built into service specifications. Then the winning price will be that which determines the best value for money.

Where services are being provided directly by the public sector, then value for money is judged by the cost of the service in comparison to the quality of service being delivered. This assessment is made by considering the following:

- *quality definitions and quality threshold benchmarks*

- *cost comparisons between other public sector providers delivering similar services*
- *comparisons between cost to the public sector for internal delivery and prices charged in the external market for similar services*
- *feedback from service recipients*
- *potential charges that could be made for the service*

Value for money will change over time in line with changes in consumer expectations; service delivery methods; relative costs; and the range of service providers. Therefore, the organisation should ensure the relative quality standards being achieved are in line with the changing nature of the service.

Summary

- The cost of quality need not be excessive, and increasing quality can sometimes be achieved at no cost
- When establishing the cost of quality, all costs need to be taken into account
- Where possible, all costs and benefits of quality improvements should be presented in monetary terms
- There are costs associated with not improving quality, such as increased complaints and waste
- A cost benefit analysis can be undertaken to help with decisions as to whether or not to invest in a particular quality improvement project
- Costs need to be broken down between one-off costs and annual recurring costs. This breakdown should also be undertaken for the benefits of quality
- Quality has to be balanced with value for money and on occasions compromises have to be made

Exercise 11

Calculating the Cost of Quality

You have been given the following information:

- ***Average cost of an employee including on-costs and overheads*** — ***£25,000***
- ***Average direct service delivery days per employee per annum*** — ***160***
- ***Average number of clients seen per month*** — ***600***
- ***Average time spent with each client per visit (assume that staff can see 3 clients per productive day)*** — ***2 hours***
- ***Average return number of visits required 50% (due to lack of information provided on the first visit)***
- ***Waiting list, 2 months equivalent***

It is recommended that to enhance quality, the average visit times be increased by 10 minutes, resulting in the need for an extra 200 days staff time per annum with the following consequences:

- ***Impact on staff time would be to increase staff numbers by 1.25 FTEs (Full Time Equivalents)***

- ***Impact on return visits required would be to reduce them to 25%***

- ***Impact on waiting list would be to reduce it down to the equivalent of 1 month***

Calculate the current cost of the service

£

Calculate the cost of the quality improvement

£

State two simple ways of reducing the above cost(s)

(i)

(ii)

Suggested solutions to this exercise can be found on page 134

Exercise 12

Cost/Benefit Analysis

Examine a service where you work or are very familiar with, and identify a potential improvement that could be made to enhance service quality.

Complete the following:

Service Description: | |
|---|

Cost of Quality Improvement

		£
e.g.	***Additional staff time***	______
	Additional training	______
	Additional equipment	______
	Improved environment	______
	Other ____________	______
	____________	______
	____________	______
	____________	______
	____________	______
	____________	______

TOTAL COST £______ ***A***

Estimate the potential monetary value of the benefits to be derived from the quality improvements.

Benefits

£

e.g. reduced staff sickness and less staff turnover (hence less recruitment costs/time) improved, morale (better productivity), etc.

____________________ __________

____________________ __________

____________________ __________

____________________ __________

____________________ __________

TOTAL BENEFITS **£________ *B***

Having calculated both the cost and the benefit, undertake some cost benefit analysis

NET COST/BENEFIT (A - B) **£ __________**

PAY BACK PERIOD **£ __________**

Given the above, do you think your idea for quality improvement is worthwhile?

Yes..

No ....

Yes with modifications.......................

Chapter 7

Obtaining Recognised Quality Standards

To facilitate the process of developing quality management systems, many organisations have gained, or seek to gain, recognised quality standards. In the UK the most common include ISO9000 (a family of standards representing an international consensus on good quality management practices), ISO14000, (environmental quality management systems), Customer Service Excellence (a standard that replaces the UK Charter Marks), Investors In People (IIP), and so on.

None of these standards conflict with each other, however, each organisation, and sometimes an individual service area, should consider which quality standard will be most beneficial in achieving their quality and business objectives. The key elements of two of the most popular quality kite marks are discussed in the following paragraphs:

- ⇨ ISO 9000
- ⇨ Investors In People (IIP)

ISO 9000

ISO stands for the International Standards Organisation and ISO 9000 is an internationally recognised family of quality standards for good management practice. It is not unusual for ISO 9000 to be a requirement when tendering to provide goods and services in the public sector. The focus of the standard is on the organisation.

ISO 9001:2008 is the standard that provides a set of standardised requirements for a quality management system, regardless of what the user organisation does, its size, or whether it is in the private or public sector. This is the most common standard of the ISO 9000 family. ISO9004:2009 relates to managing for the sustained success of an organisation – a quality management approach. This is also a relevant standard for public and third sector organisations.

The ISO9001:2008 standard provides a tried and tested framework for taking a systematic approach to managing the organisation's processes, so that they consistently turn out product that satisfies customers' expectations. This standard is achieved by the organisation meeting 5 sets of requirements, each of which has a number of areas that must be demonstrated. It is usual for an organisation to be independently audited against these criteria by a certification body, who can then issue a certificate of conformity.

A Summary of the standard

GENERAL REQUIREMENTS	
Develop your QMS*	Document your QMS*

MANAGEMENT REQUIREMENTS					
Show your commit-ment to quality	**Focus on customers**	**Support your quality policy**	**Carry out your QMS Planning**	**Allocate QMS responsibility and authority**	**Perform QM managemen reviews**

RESOURCE REQUIREMENTS			
Provide required QMS resources	**Provide competent QMS personnel**	**Provide necessary infrastructure**	**Provide suitable work environment**

REALISATION REQUIREMENTS					
Control product realisation planning	**Control customer related processes**	**Control your product design and development**	**Control purchasing and purchased products**	**Control production and service provision**	**Control monitoring and measuring equipment**

REMEDIAL REQUIREMENTS				
Establish monitoring and measurement processes	**Carry out monitoring and measurement activities**	**Identify and control nonconforming products**	**Collect and analyse quality management data**	**Make improvements and take remedi actions**

*QMS = *Quality Management System* - a set of interrelated or interacting elements that organizations use to direct and control how quality policies are implemented and quality objectives are achieved.

The advantages to be gained by service providers in obtaining this standard are summarised as follows:

- *Ensures all aspects of service delivery are documented, and hence requires thought about exactly what the service is, how it is delivered, and the standards that need to be achieved*
- *Provides a framework for regular auditing of the system and hence more effective monitoring*
- *Requires services to be delivered in a consistent manner at all times*
- *Gives more credibility to quality assertions made when tendering for work – some public sector services are competitively delivered*
- *May give confidence to the customer/user that the published standards for service delivery have been validated*
- *Provides an opportunity for an independent assessor to establish that the quality system and supporting processes and procedures are in place, and operational*

In attempting to attain and maintain an ISO9000 standard, there are a number of potential difficulties that need to be taken into account. These are:

- *It may be expensive as certification has to be paid for*
- *It may be very time consuming, particularly for services that do not already have some systems in place*
- *It concentrates on the existing service and how it is delivered (which does not necessarily mean that the service currently reaches the required standard)*

- *It may result in more form filling, data collection and increased bureaucracy*
- *Some staff may find it too inflexible given the nature of the service, resulting in a loss of creativity and an inability to use professional discretion where necessary*

These difficulties can be overcome, but it should be remembered that ISO9000 standards are not necessarily a recognition of "high quality" service. It recognises that there is a quality management system in place that is being implemented effectively. It reflects the quality standards defined by the organisation. It cannot be used to compare the service delivered by one organisation with another, as both could have an ISO9000 kite mark but deliver very different quality services.

Investors in People

Born out of the recession of the early 1990s, Investors in People was launched to produce a framework which would help organisations become more effective, by developing and harnessing the skills of their people to achieve the organisation's goals. This standard therefore has a people focus.

The mission of Investors in People is:

> "*to provide a simple and flexible framework to helping organisations of all sizes and sectors to improve their business performance.*"

This mission is achieved through the Investors in People framework which is versatile, flexible, non-prescriptive and outcome-based. The framework for business improvement sets out 10 areas which need to be met to a satisfactory level, and these are independently assessed based on evidence requirements. These requirements are clearly set out on the Investors in People website. Evidence needs to be apparent at the top manager level, the manager level (which includes top managers) and the people level (which includes top managers and managers).

The 10 key aspects of the framework, which all need to be evidenced over a range of different criteria, are summarised as follows:

01	**BUSINESS STRATEGY**	*A strategy for improving the performance of the organisation is clearly defined and understood*
02	**LEARNING AND DEVELOPMENT STRATEGY**	*Learning and development is planned to achieve the organisation's objectives*
03	**PEOPLE MANAGEMENT STRATEGY**	*Strategies for managing people are designed to promote equality of opportunity*
04	**LEADERSHIP AND MANAGEMENT STRATEGY**	*The capabilities managers need to lead, manage and develop people effectively, are clearly defined and understood*

05	**MANAGEMENT EFFECTIVENESS**	*Managers are effective in leading, managing and developing people*
06	**RECOGNITION AND REWARD**	*People's contribution to the organisation is recognised and valued*
07	**INVOLVEMENT AND EMPOWERMENT**	*People are encouraged to take ownership and responsibility by being involved in decision making*
08	**LEARNING AND DEVELOPMENT**	*People learn and develop effectively*
09	**PERFORMANCE MEASUREMENT**	*Investment in people improves the performance of the organisation*
10	**CONTINUOUS IMPROVEMENT**	*Improvements are continually made to the way people are managed and developed*

(Investors in People 2010)

The advantages of Investors in People to public sector organisations can be summarised as follows:

- *It can apply to every type of service within the public sector because it focuses on people*
- *It provides a framework to bring together many of the activities already taking place within the organisation*

- *It provides an action plan to fill the gaps that may exist within the areas of development and training*
- *It should provide a morale boost for staff at all levels and result in greater productivity and commitment*
- *It should result in better planning and improved communication throughout the organisation*
- *It can be used as a catalyst for change, especially addressing areas such as attitude and commitment to organisational goals*

There may be potential difficulties with IIP and these are summarised as follows:

- *May be expensive and is most definitely time consuming if done properly*
- *Some believe it to be a management exercise and not translated into real action for the staff (verifiers do try and check that this is not the case)*
- *It requires constant review and independent assessment every 3 years*
- *It has an inward focus and does not take into account external factors and constraints which may impact on the way in which the organisation invests in it's people*
- *Obtaining participation and involvement of all staff may prove difficult without proper coordination, and may be variable throughout the organisation*

These difficulties can be overcome with proper planning and real commitment from the top management of the organisation.

Comparisons between ISO9000 and IIP

When looking at the two quality standards, it should be emphasised that they are complementary and not conflicting.

IIP	***ISO9000***
• **Generic – All organisations hope to meet assessment criteria.**	• Individual – In so far as it recognises that an organisation has a QMS in place that it adheres to. However, the system is not benchmarked in any way and cannot be used as a comparison.
• **Concentrates on people and their contribution to achieving organisational objectives.**	• Concentrates on systems to ensure that the product/service consistently meets set standards.
• **Ideal for service businesses which are very dependent on people for the delivery of services.**	• Ideal for manufacturing companies that depend on effective systems to ensure products have zero defects.

Both standards do have things in common:

- *They are all assessed independently by external bodies*
- *The awards are usually difficult to obtain*
- *All expect continuous quality improvement*
- *If the award is achieved it has to be regularly audited*
- *The award is not automatically renewed, and can be taken away if standards have not been maintained*

All recognitions of quality are complementary to each other as they have a fundamental objective of quality improvement. There is no reason why an organisation should not seek to obtain as many quality kite marks as possible.

Summary

- ISO9000 concentrates on quality management systems and has 5 major requirements, which have several subsections that need to be met. ISO9001:2008 has been developed so that all types of organisation can seek to achieve the standard
- Investors in People has a framework of 10 criteria which need to be evidenced at all levels within the organisation. This includes top managers, managers, and all personnel. An Investor in People ensures everyone understands how they contribute to the achievement of organisational objectives
- All quality standards are worthwhile, however, each organisation must assess which are the most relevant to their development as a quality organisation delivering quality services
- It is quite common for organisations to be required to have some form of quality standard, particularly if they are required to tender for work in a competitive environment

Exercise 13

Do You Meet the Standard?

Assessment 1 – Systems and Procedures

Complete the following questionnaire in relation to your service/organisation. Tick yes, no or partly in relation to each question.

		Yes	Partly	No
1.	*Do you have a policy with respect to quality and what it means for the service/organisation?*			
2.	*Do all staff delivering the service understand the quality policy?*			
3.	*Is there a person with specific responsibility for quality?*			
4.	*Is there a senior manager with specific responsibility for quality?*			
5.	*Does the senior management team discuss quality on a regular basis at team meetings?*			
6.	*Are there written instructions with respect to how services should be delivered (i.e. quality manuals)?*			

	Yes	Partly	No
7. *Do these instructions cover all areas from inputs to outcomes, as well as details of the process?*			
8. *Are there standards developed for each aspect of service delivery?*			
9. *Are there performance indicators for each aspect of these standards?*			
10. *Are performance indicators measured and monitored on a regular basis?*			
11. *Is there a quality plan in existence setting out what needs to be done and how quality will be monitored and continuously improved?*			
12. *Is there a co-ordinated procedure for collecting, collating and feeding back information on quality attainment?*			
13. *Do you maintain a file of quality records?*			
14. *Are there regular quality audits and audit reports?*			
15. *Are exceptions to quality standards investigated and resolved?*			

	Yes	Partly	No
16. *Are exceptions to quality standards regularly reported and shared with staff?*			
17. *Are quality manuals updated on a regular basis, and staff inducted on the updates?*			
18. *Is there a staff training plan?*			
19. *Do staff receive regular training?*			
20. *Are you happy with the administration in respect of all aspects of the service (includes record keeping, filing, accuracy, completeness etc.)?*			

Assessment 2 – Personnel and Training

Complete the following questionnaire in relation to your service/organisation. Tick yes, no or partly in relation to each question.

	Yes	**Partly**	**No**
1. *Has there been a commitment from the top of the organisation (or service) to becoming an Investor in People?*			
2. *Is there a business plan in existence?*			
3. *Do all staff know and understand the objectives of the service/ organisation?*			
4. *Is there an objective in respect of staff training and development?*			
5. *Are all staff aware of who is responsible for training and development?*			
6. *Have specific resources been set aside for staff training and development (financial, physical, and time)?*			
7. *Are staff encouraged to acquire recognised qualifications?*			
8. *Do staff show a willingness to participate in training?*			

	Yes	Partly	No
9. *Is there a comprehensive induction process?*			
10. *Are managers involved in the training and development of their staff?*			
11. *Are managers assessed on their ability to train and develop their staff?*			
12. *Is there an appraisal system that covers all levels of staff?*			
13. *Does the appraisal system identify training needs?*			
14. *Are staff encouraged to request training for their own or team development?*			
15. *Are there any incentives for staff if they undergo training?*			
16. *Is there a regular review of training needs for the organisation as a whole?*			
17. *Is there a monitoring system in place to assess the impact of training?*			
18. *Is training discussed with staff before they participate in it, to ensure that it is appropriate to their needs and to identify the expected outcomes as a result of the training?*			

		Yes	Partly	No
19.	*Is the outcome of training assessed after six months, in order to identify whether or not there has been an impact on job performance and the achievement of service/ organisational objectives?*			
20.	*Is the training evaluation data used to update business plans and training plans?*			

Suggested solutions to this exercise can be found on page 136

Chapter 8

Implementing Quality

Difficulties and Solutions

The practical side of implementing quality systems is often fraught with difficulties, and many organisations have an uphill task when trying to become a "quality organisation". Some of the most common difficulties have been identified below:

- *Lack of financial and physical resources to implement quality systems, e.g. very little budget for training and developing staff*
- *Lack of expertise and understanding around quality issues and the measures required to create a truly quality driven organisation*
- *Historically poor service delivery in some areas, and lack of benchmarks against which to set quality improvements*
- *Service users not always seen as customers and hence a lack of customer focus for some public sector services*
- *Low quality image set in the minds of the consumer/public*

- *Assumptions that the drive towards value for money results in lower quality*
- *Sometimes low morale amongst staff and few ways of providing incentives*

Some practical solutions that may solve these difficulties include:

- *Obtaining external support from organisations or individuals that support quality initiatives, who are often prepared to help organisations to achieve Investors in People, sometimes at low or subsidised cost*
- *Where possible, ensuring that quality improvements can be linked to value for money initiatives and are therefore self-financing, i.e. quantifiable savings can be made as a result of the changes introduced*
- *Having a timetable for quality improvements which allows costs to be spread over a number of years, but which does not become disjointed leading to fragmentation in the quality process*
- *Recruiting volunteers to assist with environmental and other development projects; support services to enhance the customer experience; and create added value*
- *Through training and development, changing the culture within the organisation to reflect the level of service quality required*
- *Undertaking in-house, on-the-job training on issues that will promote quality such as customer care, telephone manner, dealing with the public, service knowledge and so on.*

- *Letting staff develop their own quality procedures, and manuals*
- *Working with organisations that have already implemented quality initiatives and learning from their successes and failures*
- *Developing quality definitions and standards which involve everyone, using the starting point of "what makes the service satisfactory for the users, staff and the organisation"*
- *Establishing a marketing campaign that promotes the organisation's attitude to quality and the changes that are being made. This should include details of the quality standards for the service, in a way that the public appreciate and understand*
- *Ensuring that some of the quality enhancements are physically noticeable to the consumer, such as ensuring waiting areas are clean, tidy, and comfortable, and a pro-active approach is taken in developing advocates for the service*
- *Promoting positive feedback received by staff and giving praise at every opportunity*
- *Giving staff recognition for being successful in the way they promote quality and deliver quality services to the public*

Many government departments and public organisations generally are becoming more focused on quality, and this is demonstrated by the customer service standards which many publish. The customer service standards set out a range of quality standards that customers may expect with regard to how aspects of the service are delivered. The most common areas that are covered include:

How to make contact with the service
(by telephone, email, on-line forms, or at their premises)

Answering calls
(either within a certain time, number of rings, or "promptly")

Dealing with correspondence and emails
(usually within a set number of days)

Making appointments
(usually within a time limit)

Responding to applications
(usually within a time limit)

Confidentiality and the way you can expect to be treated
(terms used usually include: helpful, responsive, courteous, etc.)

Monitoring and feedback
(usually satisfaction forms or other methods of customer feedback)

Complaints procedures
(usually clearly set out either on a website or leaflet)

With all the above areas there is no set level of quality standard across central government departments and certainly not across public sector organisations generally. Each organisation can set its own targets, but they must then deliver against them. Most organisations publish results as to how well their service standards have been met. This gives the public information on which to judge the organisation's performance and helps to set targets for quality improvement.

Key Steps

The key steps to effective quality implementation can be summarised as follows:

- *Commitment to quality must come from the top and be on-going, i.e. not a one off project*
- *Ensure quality improvement programmes are not confused with cost-cutting/savings initiatives*
- *Staff are involved throughout the whole process of quality development, with leadership coming from the top and detailed implementation from the bottom-up*
- *Customers, users, stakeholders, and the public need to be involved throughout the process, with constant consultation and feedback*
- *Continual training and development around areas of quality throughout the process of implementation and afterwards*
- *Understand that quality does not stand still and therefore the organisation needs to be striving for continuous improvement in all areas*
- *Each year standards need to be made public along with the results of the measurement and monitoring*
- *Realistic timetables need to be set such that quality can really be achieved and not be superficial. This may take a number of years to*

ensure a quality culture is embedded throughout the organisation

It should be remembered that every organisation is different and therefore the solution to implementing quality will be different in each case.

Exercise 14

Action Plan

Thinking about all the areas of the book:

- ➔ What is Quality?
- ➔ Setting Quality Standards
- ➔ Measuring and Monitoring Quality
- ➔ Quality Management
- ➔ Investing in Quality
- ➔ Obtaining Recognised Quality Standards
- ➔ Implementing Quality

Consider what actions need to be taken in order to improve your service in each of these areas, and what actions you personally intend to take

	How can my service area improve?	***What actions can I take?***
What is Quality?		

	How can my service area improve?	**What actions can I take?**
Setting Quality Standards		
Measuring and Monitoring		
Quality Management		

	How can my service area improve?	***What actions can I take?***
Investing in Quality		
Obtaining Recognised Quality Standards		
Implementing Quality		

Solutions to Exercises

Solutions to Exercises

Solution to Exercise 1

Values and Objectives: Impact on Quality

For the following example, set out what you consider to be:

a) The most important values

b) The key strategic objectives

c) The impact on quality

A person who buys a Rolls Royce

VALUES:

- Reliability
- Investment
- Durability
- Safety
- Image

OBJECTIVE:

- To own a high specification car that holds its value and projects an image of prosperity

IMPACT ON QUALITY:

- High expectations of performance
- High levels of customer care
- Zero defects

A person who buys a small family car

VALUES:

- Economy
- Practicality
- Environment

OBJECTIVE:

- To own a vehicle that gets one from A to B

IMPACT ON QUALITY:

- Basic good all round performance
- Low maintenance costs

Solution to Exercise 2

Service Quality Definitions

Public Sector Values

1) *Value for money*
2) *Community*
3) *Environment*
4) *Efficiency*
5) *Equality*

Quality Definition for School Bus Service

A value for money, and environmentally friendly bus service for **all** the community

Private Sector Values

1) *Profit*
2) *Efficiency*
3) *Cost Effectiveness*
4) *Customer Care*
5) *Image*

Quality Definition for School Bus Service

A cost effective and profitable school bus service that meets our customers' requirements

Solution to Exercise 4

Quality Standards

Insert your public sector definition for the School Bus Service from Exercise 2, then set a number of quality standards that you would be prepared to put on show to the general public.

Quality Definition

A value for money, and environmentally friendly bus service for all the community

Quality Standards

Tangible:

⇨ Keeping within x minutes of the time table

⇨ Achieving average journey times between stops

⇨ Achieving minimum waiting times for passengers at stops

⇨ Visiting all schools on the route

⇨ Keeping vehicles maintained and below a certain age

Intangible:

- Pleasant and clean environment on the bus
- Polite and helpful drivers
- Customer satisfaction rating of x%
- Safety record
- Implementing equal opportunities policies

Solution to Exercise 6

Performance Indicators

For each standard identified in Exercise 4, list at least two performance indicators (think about how they might be measured).

Standard	Performance Indicators	Measurement
Keeping within x minutes of the timetable	*Times of arrival at the stop*	*Time log – daily*
	Times of departure from the stop	*Time log – daily*
Achieving average journey times between stops	*Times of departure from one stop*	*Time log – daily*
	Times of arrival at the following stop	*Time log – daily*
Achieving minimum waiting times for passengers at stops	*Times between buses arriving at each stop*	*Time log – daily*
	Passenger feedback on their waiting time	*Customer/user survey – every six months*

Standard	Performance Indicators	Measurement
Visiting all schools on the route	*Time of arrival at each stop*	*Time log – daily*
	Feedback from schools on the route	*Schools survey – every six months*
Keeping vehicles maintained and below a certain age	*Number of breakdowns*	*Record of each breakdown and the impact immediately logged in breakdown book*
	Age of vehicles	*Date of vehicle purchase for all vehicles in use*
Pleasant and clean environment	*Litter levels*	*Bus inspection – daily*
	Feedback from users	*Customer/user survey – every six months*
Polite and helpful drivers	*Number of complaints*	*No. of complaints registered in complaints book*
	Feedback from users	*Customer/user survey – every six months*

Standard	Performance Indicators	Measurement
Customer satisfaction rating of x%	*Number of complaints*	*No. of complaints registered in complaints book*
	Feedback from users	*Customer/user survey – every six months*
Implementing equal opportunities policies	*Number of complaints*	*No. of complaints registered in complaints book*
	Feedback from users	*Customer/user survey – every six months*

Solution to Exercise 7

Measuring Performance

Given the scenarios provided, note down the following for each case.

a) Is this a quality Service?

Case 1

Yes, in the eyes of the provider. No, in the eyes of the customer; therefore for a customer focused organisation, the answer should be no.

Case 2

Yes, as the specification is met and the specification sets the quality definitions and standards.

Case 3

Unclear because the service manager appears to be content with the service and only has the view of one employee. Further investigation would need to take place in order to establish the position. However, certain practices if true, would be considered poor.

b) What type of performance measurement would you undertake?

Case 1

Accuracy and customer satisfaction survey.

Case 2

Inspection of rubbish levels between emptying times, and local resident satisfaction survey.

Case 3
Real waiting times, i.e. when someone gets seen, and customer satisfaction survey.

c) How could the service be improved?

Case 1
Better consultation with the customer (managers) to establish what they consider the quality standards ought to be. Develop the service quality accordingly.

Case 2
Evaluation of the specification in the light of local feedback from satisfaction surveys and complaints. Revised specification for next tendering round to reflect the evaluation results.

Case 3
Ensuring all staff are adequately trained and adhering to a quality manual which sets out clearly how each aspect of the service should be delivered in order to meet the quality standards. Closer monitoring by the manager, and evaluation of customer feedback/satisfaction with the overall service.

Solution to Exercise 9
Total Quality Management in Practice

Some of the actions the manager could undertake to develop a TQM system are given below (note these are not in any order of priority)

- *Produce a mission statement*
- *Introduce staff appraisals and performance management*
- *Select a TQM team including staff and representation from users*
- *Paint the common parts*
- *Introduce procedures manuals for all areas of work, setting standards, targets and monitoring procedures*
- *Change current caterers, and issue new guidelines on menus*
- *Set out objectives for the next five years which identify quality improvements*
- *Make a commitment to becoming an Investor in People*
- *Develop a corporate logo and use throughout the organisation*
- *Introduce activities such as film making, fitness training, and an educational programme*

- *Undertake a satisfaction survey amongst users and request suggestions for improvements*
- *Undertake a staff survey and request suggestions for improvements*
- *Undertake a visitors survey and request suggestions for improvements*
- *Implement a staff training programme*
- *Develop regular meetings with users and visitors*
- *Make the visiting areas more comfortable, include new drinks machine, etc.*
- *Obtain a quality accreditation*
- *Hold regular staff meetings*
- *Appoint a new independent person to deal with complaints and to audit quality systems*
- *Arrange an annual open day*

Solution to Exercise 11

Calculating the Cost of Quality

You have been given the following information:

■ *Average cost of an employee including on-costs and overheads*	*£25,000*
■ *Average direct service delivery days given by employee per annum*	*160*
■ *Average number of clients seen per month*	*600*
■ *Average time spent with each client per visit (assume that staff can see 3 clients per productive day)*	*2 hours*
■ *Average return number of visits required 50% (due to lack of information provided on the first visit)*	
■ *Waiting list 2 months equivalent*	

It is recommended that to enhance quality, the average visit times be increased by 10 minutes, resulting in the need for an extra 200 days staff time per annum

- *Impact on staff time would be to increase staff numbers by 1.25 FTEs*
- *Impact on return visits required would be to reduce them to 25%*
- *Impact on waiting list would be to reduce it down to 1 month equivalent*

The current cost of the service (staff only) | **£375,000***

* *200 productive days per month required to see 600 clients per month, because only 3 clients can be seen in one productive staff day.*

200 x 12 = 2,400 productive days per annum required to see all the clients.

Each staff member currently delivers 160 productive days per annum.

Therefore, it will take 15 staff members to deliver the 2,400 days (2,400 ÷ 160)

The cost is therefore £375,000 (15 x 25,000)

The cost of the quality improvement | **£31,250****

** *(£25,000 x 1.25)*

Two simple ways of reducing the above cost of quality:

(i) Increase the number of direct delivery days worked by each member of staff by 14 days per year to 174 days. This would absorb the extra 200 days required without extra staff costs.

(ii) Review the way in which the service is being delivered and consider alternative ways. For example, using technology may lead to greater efficiency and yield an opportunity for reducing costs.

Solution to Exercise 13

Do You Meet the Standard?

Award yourself the following points for each question:

Yes	**=**	**2 points**
Partly	**=**	**1 point**
No	**=**	**0 points**

Assessment 1 – Systems and Procedures

Points scored: Under 20

Although this is a low score, it does not mean that the service being delivered is of poor quality. The score reflects the lack of formalisation in the way in which services are currently delivered, along with a general lack of documentation and record keeping. It may be that your service does not lend itself well to structures and systems. However, there is merit at trying to at least put in place some of the key elements required for ISO 9000, such as service standards and procedure manuals, even if you consider that achieving the standard is not appropriate for your service/organisation.

Points Scored: 20 to 29

This is an average score, and not surprising for many public service providers who have not fully embarked on the path to becoming a quality organisation. This score indicates that there are elements in existence that can be used to help in the development of a quality system, and hence provide a starting point for ISO 9000. The next stage is to prepare a comprehensive action plan identifying where the gaps are and how these can be filled. This may take some time, and if ISO 9000 is a goal then your service/organisation should have a realistic timetable for its achievement, at least a year.

Points Scored: 30 to 40

This score indicates that you should have very little difficulty in preparing for quality standards such as ISO 9000. However, if you have not scored yes to questions 6 to 10 and number 17 there may still be a lot of work to be done in order to be confident that you are adequately prepared to be assessed for the standard. Even if you do not wish to go through the process of gaining accreditation, it is still worthwhile aiming to eliminate any no answers such that you can be assured you have the system in place to achieve the level of quality desired by your service/organisation.

Assessment 2 – Personnel and Training

You may find that your scores are very different to the previous self assessment results for ISO 9000. This may affect which standard you wish to achieve first.

Points Scored: Under 20

Given that staff are very important to the delivery of most public sector services, this is a low score that needs to be addressed even if your service/organisation does not wish to acquire a recognised standard such as Investors in People. As a matter of good practice, there should be certain basic processes in place such as appraisals and training plans. It is unlikely that staff will perform to the best of their abilities if no effort is being put into their training and development. It makes good sense in terms of quality and value for money to ensure that investing in staff is linked to the achievement of organisational goals.

Points Scored: 20 to 29

This is an average score, and indicates that there may be some fundamental elements missing from the current organisation's training and development processes. This may be in the area of business planning, where staff are not aware of the organisation's objectives and the contribution they should be making towards their achievement, or it may mean that there is no appraisal system in place for all staff. If there are gaps of this nature, then there will be a reasonable amount of work required to meet a recognised standard such as Investors in People and hence a realistic time scale needs to be adopted for its achievement, at least a year.

Points Scored: 30 to 40

This score indicates that your organisation has most of the required processes in place in order to achieve a recognised quality standard such as Investors in People. Most organisations at this stage find continuous evaluation to be the most difficult area to address. Although training and development is well established, the impact is often not thoroughly tested and examined over the long term. If this is a weak area, it may be worth investing in some assistance in identifying the most appropriate method of evaluating training for your service/organisation. It is worthwhile developing an action plan which identifies how any outstanding issues will be implemented within a specific time frame.

INDEX

A

B

C

D

E

G

I

K

L

M

O

P

Q

R

S

T

For further information see www.hbpublications.com
and www.fci-system.com

www.ingramcontent.com/pod-product-compliance
Lightning Source LLC
Chambersburg PA
CBHW070733220326
41598CB00024BA/3404